Running for Beginners

A guide to successful running for health, fitness and pleasure

K P Foster

Contents

Introduction

I want to thank you for buying the book, *"**Running for Beginners: A guide to successful running for health, fitness and pleasure**"*.

Everyone knows how to run, one step in front of the other at a faster pace than walking. But running for fitness involves a lot more than the basic movement of your feet. One of the most common reasons novice runners give up during the early stages is that they take this simplistic approach to it and end up injured and in pain.

Whether your goal is fitness, pleasure or tackling a marathon for charity, there are a few key factors that must first be introduced to become a successful runner.

- Warming up your muscles before a run
- Cooling down your muscles after a run
- Wearing the correct footwear
- Distance – planning your run so that you do not overstretch yourself
- Fluid intake – regular hydration
- Clothing – appropriate clothing for health, hydration and optimum benefit
- Time limits – starting small
- Nutrition – fuelling your body
- Running anxiety – how to overcome self consciousness

Before starting a running regime, all these factors and more must be addressed. The aim of this book is to teach you how to make your running experience both successful and fun.

Thanks again for downloading this book, I hope you enjoy it!

Chapter 1 - Getting Started

Running Anxiety

Many people suffer from a feeling of self-consciousness when they begin running. Whether you are out on the streets, in a park or using a treadmill at a gym, the idea of looking silly often creeps into the conscious thoughts of a novice runner. This is perfectly normal but it is important to acknowledge that even the most professional of runners was once a novice.

People feel pleasure when they see others experiencing things they are passionate about, and it is rare someone won't offer encouragement to another person when they see them doing what they themselves love.

Despite the fact that running can be a competitive sport, runners are no different in their encouragement of others and, no matter what your motivation for the run, they will respect and acknowledge you if they encounter you when they are out and about.

In any endeavour, it is easy to feel intimidated by someone who is more experienced than you, but you will find that very few people won't chat with you during a run and they will be happy to answer any questions you have. There is no judgment of technique or ability, just an honest interest in giving advice and extending your knowledge.

Public places seem to be the most worrisome for a novice runner. Occasionally you may encounter a group of people who will taunt you, but that same group of people will taunt anyone irrespective of what they are doing and should be ignored. Most non runners are so busy with their own lives that they will either acknowledge you with a smile or ignore you completely. If asked later in the day they will likely not even remember having seen you.

Keep focused on why you are running and what you are achieving. Two excellent distraction techniques are:

1. Running with a friend; you are less likely to be aware of others around you if you are with someone else, especially if that person is also relatively new to running

2. Music; one of the best accompaniments to running is an ipod. Firstly, you can run in time with the music. Make yourself a playlist of songs to run to. This will lift your mood and help to motivate you. Secondly, you are focusing on the music that is playing and that will distract you from noticing the people around you.

If you find your mind drifting into an anxious state about what others think when they see you running, re-focus on the music that is playing and before you know it, all else will be firmly in the background. Lastly, listening to music will stop you monitoring yourself. Concentrating on how far you have run and how tired you are will affect your psychological state and make you feel tired and achy long before your body really feels those things.

Health

If you have never exercised before, or if it is a long time since you have done anything physically taxing, you may find you have an unrealistic view of your general fitness levels.

Similarly, some medical conditions can also impact on your overall health and fitness, so when starting to run you will need to take these things into consideration so you do not overdo it and cause yourself injuries.

Doing too much too soon can also result in the loss of motivation for running so take it easy to begin with and don't expect too much of yourself. Any distance a beginner runs is an achievement and over time, as your fitness levels increase, the running can be adapted to suit your current health.

If you can relate to any of the following, I would advise that you seek advice from your doctor before you start to run. This does not mean you are unable to run; it is simply to ensure you can prevent any common associated problems.

- Pregnancy
- High Blood Pressure
- Diabetes
- Heart Disease
- Over 50 with no recent exercise
- Any muscular diseases
- Chest pains
- Obesity

Fluid Intake

It is a widespread myth that drinking water while running will cause a side stitch. In reality, lack of hydration while running is a cause of muscle cramps, headaches, fatigue, exhaustion and heat related issues.

Drink 1 pint of water about an hour before you plan to start running. The intervening time will give your body an opportunity to void any excess fluids your body is storing.

Right before your run you can drink up to an additional half a pint of water. (Much more than this and you will need to stop for frequent toilet breaks).

This amount is sufficient to give your body enough hydration for the physical exercise you will be giving it. (Do not go running with a hangover, your body is already dehydrated and you will suffer cramps and possibly other injuries).

Take water with you when you run. Some people carry a bottle but I find it easier to take a water pouch with a drinking tube attached that I can strap to my body.

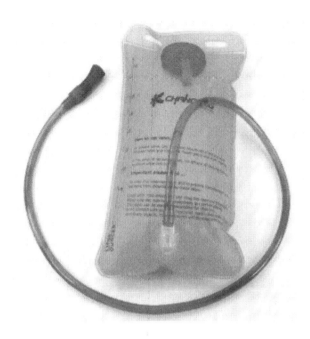

Make sure you do not over-hydrate as this can lead to fluid retention and abnormally low salt levels. The trick to drinking while running is to only take a drink when you are thirsty. If you stick to drinking around a quarter of a pint every 20 – 30 minutes this should be sufficient to keep your body well hydrated.

Once you are more experienced, and if you have increased your running time to more than 75 minutes, you will need to include a sports drink that contains carbohydrates, sodium and electrolytes to replace any lost minerals and sodium.

At the end of your run, once you have warmed down, dink between half a pint and a pint of water to fully rehydrate your system.

Distance

How far should I run is a regular question asked by the novice runner; the simple answer is 'as far as your body wants you to'. When you first start you will need to account for your fitness levels so it is a good idea to map a route and do not overdo it.

Decide where you want to run – Are you running on pavements, across fields in the park or on a running track?

Plan a route - start yourself off with around 10 – 20 minutes at most. Many runners start with a ten minute run to build up their stamina and fitness.

Begin with a small route and don't worry if you can't complete it all. If you begin to feel it is too much, slow your pace, this is not a race. If you need to, walk the rest of the way. Keep in mind, 10 – 20 minutes does not seem a long amount of time but for someone unused to exercise, this is equivalent to an athlete working out for an extra half hour at least – so acknowledge your accomplishment.

Over time you will be able to comfortably run for a much longer period. The golden rule is to stop and walk when your body tells you it has done enough.

Chapter 2 - Running Injuries

As with anything physical, injuries are sometimes inevitable and they are an accepted part of the life of a runner. The difference is whether the pain you feel requires medical attention, rest or if it can be ignored.

Prevention is always better than cure so minimising the risk is a no brainer, but even with all your bases covered, sometimes you will experience some level of discomfort.

Physical exertion of any kind will lead to muscle soreness for a beginner. Previously unused muscles will protest and begin to ache but, so long as you don't push yourself beyond what your body is capable of, this can be worked through. This type of pain is reduced when you are properly prepared and wearing the correct clothing and footwear.

Usually this type of discomfort is not localised and will include muscular aches and pains. If the pain is localised to a particular area, such as a knee or ankle, and is accompanied by swelling, this can usually be helped by:

- Application of a cold compress for up to 20 minutes every 4 – 6 hours until the swelling has reduced. If you do not have a cold compress, a bag of frozen vegetables will work just as well.

- Following the compress, wrap the area in a bandage, either a support bandage or a medium to loosely wrapped bandage. (Be careful not to wrap the bandage to tight as this will affect circulation).

- Elevation – Lift the leg or affected area to above waist to chest height.

- Rest for a day or two if necessary, there is nothing to be gained by working an injury.

If the pain of your injury is higher than that of the mild injuries described above, and continues throughout your run with increasing intensity then listen to your body. While this is rarely a serious injury, if you refuse to listen to your body it will soon become one, so stop.

Apply the steps for a mild injury and let your body rest and recuperate fully.

If you experience any high levels of pain or you find you are limping, or your posture or running style have changed to accommodate a particular pain, then stop running straightaway.

If you are experiencing extensive swelling, difficulty in moving the injured area, severe pain in bones or joints, spreading pain, numbness or tingling or if the affected area is painful to touch it is always best to seek medical advice before continuing your running regime.

Running is generally associated with strength in the legs but many injuries are caused because focus is placed solely on the leg muscles. Ignoring your core muscles is asking for problems. It doesn't matter how strong your lower muscles are if you are soft and squishy in the middle. Strengthening your core muscle will provide stability throughout your body and support you while you run.

Side Stitches

A side stitch is something most of us have experienced at least once but, despite much speculation, the true cause of side stitches is still uncertain. A lot of research into the subject has provided no definitive results however there are some preventative measures which can be taken that have proved to be quite successful in reducing the occurrence of a side stitch.

- Avoid sugary drinks before running
- Do not eat within one hour of starting your run
- Ensure you are properly hydrated
- Warm up correctly
- Control your breathing while running
- Manage your posture when running
- If running in extreme cold, use a neck warmer to breathe through so your lungs are not being filled with freezing air

If you do develop a side stitch while running the most effective way of relieving it is through your breathing. By taking a deep intake of breath you will force your diaphragm downwards, hold your breath for 2 – 3 seconds then release forcefully.

You can also push down with your fingers on the area on the stitch. Press firmly but don't press too deeply, your aim is to relieve the stitch, not cause bruising.

If these methods fail, then slow down to a walk until the stitch passes.

Chapter 3 - Footwear & Clothing

Running Shoes

Wearing the correct footwear when running may seem like something that requires little thought but it is one of the most important elements. Incorrect footwear can, and will, cause injury.

When you first consider becoming a runner it is tempting to grab your old trainers, slip them on your feet and be off out of the door. This is a main factor in why people give up before they have started properly. You are putting a lot of pressure on your feet and inadequate footwear will not support you.

I understand that when you first start you may not wish to spend money on new trainers because you do not know if you will enjoy running, but you can always sell them if you decide it is not for you. Starting out ill equipped will not allow you the opportunity to see if you enjoy it or not.

Firstly you need to consider the shape of your foot. A specialist shoe store will do this for you but if you prefer to choose your footwear without recommendation you will need to recognise the type of foot you have.

High Arch Foot

People with high arches generally roll their feet outwards when they run so the running shoe needs to support this. Additionally, as you grow older, the high arch will fall slightly which will increase the size of your foot so regularly sizing is required.

To determine if you have high arches, the easiest way is through a footprint. There will be a definite arch to your foot and the footprint will show a thin foot area where the arched section is removed from the print.

For a high arched foot you will need either a flexible or cushioned running shoe. These should have a soft midsole that will absorb shock.

Neutral Foot

This is the most common foot shape and people with neutral feet generally suffer less injury. It is also much easier to choose a running shoe that will support your foot. Stay away from shoes designed for motion control or stability but most others should serve you well.

Flat Foot

Flat footed people roll their feet inward when running and this can cause quite a lot of discomfort when wearing the wrong shoe. You will require a shoe that has either stability or motion control. It is possible to acquire custom made insoles that will compensate for the flat foot but these can be expensive.

Even with the correct footwear, old or worn out shoes will still cause problems when you run. A good pair of shoes will usually last you between 300 – 400 miles depending on how heavily they are used. As soon as you start to become aware of muscle aches you do not usually suffer from it is generally time to replace your running shoe.

When running, your feet will swell so always buy shoes that are between half and one size too big to allow for this.

Clothing

The first thing people tend to think is that when running, cotton is the ideal material because it is light and lets your body breathe. Running in cotton clothing is actually a very bad idea because it is inevitable you will sweat, and cotton not only absorbs moisture but it holds onto it. Exercise and wet clothing are only compatible when you are swimming.

A technical fabric is the most suitable for physical exercise as it keeps the sweat away from the body which prevent chafing. Silk also has this quality but can be expensive.

There is a large variety of technical fabric clothing on the market with varying price ranges. Thinsulate and CoolMax are both good but any clothing made from a polypropylene material will work.

For ladies, a good sports bra is a necessity. No matter what your size, if you are unsupported you will begin to suffer discomfort. Try a few different sports bra's to ensure you have adequate support as well as comfort, and stay away from cotton. Because of the elasticity of the material, you will need to replace your sports bra after 65 – 75 washes to be sure you have adequate support.

The material of your socks is just as important, in addition to a technical fabric, socks made from polyester are ideal, these are however, quite thin so you may prefer to wear 2 pairs to help protect from blisters.

It is also important to consider the climate when you go running. In hot weather stick to light coloured clothing which will deflect rather than absorb the heat.

If you do not feel comfortable running in sunglasses, wear a visor to keep the sun from your eyes. Do not be tempted to wear a full cap as this will trap heat and can lead to your body overheating. Always remember to wear sunscreen when you are running in warm weather.

Cold weather running will require layering of your clothing. There is no point wearing a big bulky sweater just because it looks like it will keep you warm. Layering will allow warm air to become trapped between the layers while still allowing moisture to be directed away from your skin.

A good sports tee-shirt beneath a climate control, waterproof tracksuit jacket is both comfortable and will allow you freedom of movement while keeping you warm. In extreme cold a middle layer of non cotton fleece can be added.

For your bottom half, add a base layer sports leggings or tights with a waterproof outer layer.

Add a warm hat, a neck gaiter and gloves to ensure optimal comfort.

Caring for your clothing

Because the fabric of your sports clothing removes sweat from your body, they can soon become full of smelly bacteria which no amount of washing will remove.

To avoid this, always wash with a detergent which is specially designed for technical fabrics. This will remove any bacteria and smell while keeping the technical qualities of the fabric intact. Wash running wear in cold water and never dry in an electric dryer.

Chapter 4 – Warm Up & Cool Down

Before you start any run, no matter how experienced you are, warming up is vital if you want to avoid serious injuries. Muscles need to be warm to allow for flexibility and optimum muscle performance. By completing warm up exercises prior to your running you allow the blood vessels to dilate, this supplies your muscles with plenty of much needed oxygen. Warm up also has the added benefit of raising your heart rate slightly and so preparing your body for more exercise. Starting cold can result in torn muscles, shortness of breath and stress on your heart health.

In much the same way, a warm down must be completed to slow down your heart rate and relax your muscles after a run.

Warming Up

Although your muscles will benefit from stretching it is a bad idea to start off with stretching exercise before your muscles have been warmed up. Start off with 5 minutes of cardio/aerobic exercise to get things moving. Star jumps are a great 1st exercise as this covers the aerobic element and prepares your body for stretching.

Start off with 30 star jumps, rest for 30 seconds and do another 30. Do not rush this exercise. A steady pace is much more effective than rushing through 30 jumps incorrectly.

1. Start with your knees bent slightly and your feet together. Place your arms loosely at your sides.
2. Jump opening your legs to shoulder width apart while raising your hands up above your head. Try to complete this in as smooth a motion as possible.
3. You should land with your arms above your head and your legs in line with your shoulders with your knees straight.
4. Jump again and bring your arms, legs and knees back to the starting position.

As well as getting your blood pumping and warming up your muscles, this exercise will help to loosed hips, pelvis, shoulders and ankles.

Once you have warmed your muscles slightly start your stretching exercises.

You may already know some stretching exercises but here is an example of a few which are effective.

Stretch 1

1. Stand with hands on hips and feet shoulder width apart.
2. Straighten your back and tense your stomach muscles.
3. Lift your left leg straight out in front of you to 90° (or as high as is comfortable)
4. Extend your left arm straight behind you and your right arm straight out in front of you.
5. Twist from the waist and try to touch your left toes with your right hand.
6. Hold for 3 seconds and return to starting position.
7. Repeat with right leg
8. Complete a repetition of 6 to 10 per leg

Stretch 2

1. Place your arms in a boxing stance in front of your chest.
2. Place legs should width apart.
3. Twist left from your waist and lift your left leg, knee bent.
4. Touch your right elbow to your left knee.
5. Repeat on opposite side.
6. Complete a repetition of 5 – 10 per leg

Stretch 3

- Hold arms straight out to the sides and place your feet slightly wider than shoulder width apart.
- Twist from the waist and bring your left arm down to touch your right toe. Your right arm should be kept straight and will now be pointing upwards.
- Turn your neck to look at the fingers of your right hand.
- Return to starting position and repeat on the opposite side.
- Complete a repetition of 6 – 10 on each side.

Stretch 4

- Place legs hip width apart with your back straight.
- Place hands on hips and take a big step forward with your left leg.
- Lower your hips towards the ground until your left thigh is parallel with the floor.
- Keep your left knee level with your left heel, head straight and forward facing and hold for a count of 3.
- Return to starting position.
- Repeat for a repetition of 5 – 10 on each leg.

You are now ready to begin your run. Remember to start out with a slow jog and build it up.

Cool Down

Towards the end of your run, slow down to a slow jog for the last 5 minutes to give your muscles and heart rate time to slow and cool down.

This will help the muscles to begin to cool slowly while you are doing your post run stretches.

Lower Back Stretch
1. Place your hands and knees on the floor in a crawl position.
2. Arch your back towards the ceiling and head towards the floor, leaning backwards slightly on your legs and hold for 5 – 10 seconds.
3. Return to starting position.
4. Arch your shoulders and neck upwards and lower your stomach towards the floor and hold for 5 – 10 seconds.
5. Return to starting position and repeat 5 – 10 times.

Neck Stretch
1. Stand with your face facing forwards and neck straight.
2. Gently bed your head backwards and hold for a count of 5 – 10. (Do not bend beyond what is comfortable)
3. Return to start position.
4. Bend your head forward and hold for 5 – 10 seconds.
5. Return to start.
6. Turn your head left until your chin is level with your shoulder. Hold for 5 – 10 seconds and return to start position.
7. Repeat on the right side.
8. Complete a repetition of 5 per position.

Hamstring Stretch

1. Stand with your feet together and arms hung loosely at your sides.
2. Cross your right leg in front of your left leg so ankles are close together.
3. Keep your left leg straight and bend from the waist.
4. Clasp hands together and reach down to your toes as far as possible without it being painful.
5. Hold to 15 – 20 seconds and return to starting position.
6. Repeat with left leg for a repetition of 5.

Calf Stretch

1. Stand parallel to a wall and extend both arms, should width apart.
2. Touch wall with your hands and bend your left knee.
3. Extend your right leg behind you as far as possible and keeping your right foot flat on the floor.
4. Hold for 15 – 20 return legs to starting position.
5. Repeat with opposite leg.
6. Complete a repetition of 5 per leg.

Quadriceps Stretch (Front Thighs)

1. Stand straight with feet together.
2. Lift your left foot behind you and reach round with your left hand to hold your left foot.
3. Pull your foot in towards your bottom and hold for 15 – 20 seconds.
4. Return to starting position.
5. Repeat with the right foot.
6. Complete a repetition of 6 – 10 per leg.

Core Exercises

Arm & Leg Lift
- Lie on the floor, face down and rest your forehead on the ground.

- Extend your arms forwards on either side of your head with your legs flat and straight.

- Slowly, lift your right and your left leg as high as is comfortable. Hold for 2 – 3 seconds then gently lower to the ground.

- Repeat with your left arm and your right leg.

- Complete a repetition of 10 per arm/leg

After 2 – 3 weeks, increase to two cycles of 10 per arm/leg

Hip Bridging
- Lie face up on the floor and bend your knees. Keep the soles of your feet flat to the ground.

- Relax you arms and place them at the side of your body

- Pull in your stomach muscles and tighten your bum muscles

- Keeping your shoulders and feet on the floor, lift your hips and upper body. Try to keep your body in a straight line as you lift.

- Hold for 5 seconds then release bum and stomach muscles and slowly lower your body back to the floor.

- Complete a repetition of 10.

After 1 week, attempt to hold for 10 – 15 seconds – slowly building up to 20 -25 seconds over the coming weeks.

After 3 weeks increase to two cycles of 10

Front Plank

- Lie face down on a mat. Bend your elbows and place them level with your shoulders, forearms flat to the floor and stretched out in front of you with palms down.

- Legs should be straight and flat to the floor with feet upturned slightly so you are resting on your toes.

- Keeping your legs, shoulders and back straight, tighten your stomach muscles and push up on your elbows and toes so your body is in a straight line, angling downwards from your shoulders to your feet.

- Focus on taking slow deep breathes and hold for up to 30 seconds.

- Slowly lower your body back down to starting position.

- Repeat for a repetition of 5.

As your core muscles strengthen, increase the plank hold by 10 seconds, up to a maximum of 60 seconds.

After several weeks you can increase the difficulty by raising 1 leg for 10 seconds while in the plank position, lowering and raising the other leg.

Bicycle crunch

- Lie face upwards on the floor and bend your knees into a 90° position. Knees should be aligned with your hips. Place your hands under your head.

- Bring your left elbow and your right knee together over your chest/waist.

- Return to start position and complete the exercise with your right elbow and left knee.

- Continue without a break for 60 seconds.

After 2 weeks increase to 90 seconds

Reverse crunch

- Lie face up on the floor with your arms at your side and legs straight.

- Press down with your hands and swiftly lift both legs together, knees bent, towards your chest.

- Try to bring your legs high enough to lift your hips from the floor.
  Lower and straighten legs until they are two to three inches off the floor and hold for a count of three.

- Repeat for a repetition of 10

After 1 – 2 weeks you can extend the repetition to 15 – 20 and the count from three to between 5 and 10.

Chapter 5 – How to Run for Maximum Benefit

Everyone can run and unless you are racing through the park, kicking your legs around like a dying fly and waving your arms in the air, no one will pay any attention to you, but if you want to run in a way that is going to be of optimum benefit with a minimum of stress on your muscles, there are a few rules you need to observe.

Firstly, you need to be placing your feet correctly.

Landing on your heels will limit your momentum moving forwards and cause stress to your knees which will result in unnecessary pain.

Landing on your toes will put all the pressure onto your calves and shins which can cause serious damage to your shin bones and calf muscles. You will suffer from calf cramps and your lower leg muscles will become tired long before they should.

Toe striking can also cause you to bounce as you run which places unnecessary stress on your body and will lead to prematurely tiring along with muscular aches and tension.

The ideal landing position is the ball of your foot. You then roll forward through your toes. Keep your steps at a reasonable length and land with your foot below your body.

Keep your feet pointed straight forward. Angling your foot to one side or the other will lead to injury.

Arms should be relaxed and able to swing with your hands at hip or waist level. Allow your shoulders and neck to relax and be free of tension.

Running while your body muscles are tensed up will lead to you feeling fatigue before your body is actually tired and will cause stiffness of your back, neck and shoulder muscles which, in addition to muscular pain, will lead to headaches and a general feeling of discomfort. It will also cause your performance and stamina to suffer.

Keep your shoulders front facing and loose. If you feel them hunching forwards, push your shoulder blades together and lift your neck so your posture is erect and your chest is open so you can breathe freely. Keep your pelvis straight so your stomach is not clenched tight. Incorrect posture will cause neck and lower back pain and increase your risk of injury.

Keep your breathing steady and relaxed. Breathe in deeply through your mouth to maintain maximum oxygen levels to your muscles and breathe out through your nose. Breathe deeply from your diaphragm, using your chest to breathe results in shallow breaths with minimum oxygen intake.

Running seven days a week is not advisable as your muscles and body do require rest. This does not mean that you have to take a day off if you do not want to.

For the first 2 months, take 4 days every week for your running. Use the additional 3 days for doing core strengthening exercises. As you gain in fitness and strength, this can be adjusted to 5 days for running and two days for core strengthening work.

Chapter 6 - Nutrition

So now you are all set to become a successful runner but there is one important element that has yet to be covered - Nutrition. On average you burn around 100 calories for each mile you run so these calories need to be replenished. Additionally, you are using much more energy than normal so your carbohydrate intake must also be increased.

Your muscles are working much harder than they previously were and in order to ensure they continue to work to their optimum level you will need to consume enough protein to sustain, strengthen and repair your muscles.

Everything that you put into your body will affect the way it performs, from regular and sufficient hydration, to vitamins, minerals and dietary intake, each one is as important as the next.

The timing of your food intake is also significant. If you miss meals, binge or eat too much or too little you will not on damage you overall health but also diminish the effectiveness of your run and increase your risk of injury.

Breakfast, lunch and dinner should be eaten regularly and you should not underestimate the necessity of refuelling after a run. It is more important to eat the right foods in the correct combinations than to fill a plate with whatever is at hand.

While it is often considered better to eat convenience food rather than no food, these are rarely nutritious and will provide little to no benefit for a runner. If you have no time to prepare a good quality meal, whip up a protein and carbohydrate rich smoothly. These are particular good for post run refuelling.

(Refuelling should be done within 30 minutes after you have completed your cool down for maximum recovery benefit).

Runners should aim to balance their meals with 55 – 65% carbohydrate, 20 – 35% unsaturated fats and 10 – 35% protein.

Balanced Diet

Complex carbohydrates provide a slow release energy source and are high in fibre so, unlike fast absorption carbohydrates, they allow the release of energy in a steady stream so you can avoid the highs and lows that result from blood sugar spikes.

Your main carbohydrate intake should be from complex Carbs however, pre and post run meals should include low fibre carbohydrate sources (simple Carbs) to give you an energy boost. Try to limit the intake of processed Carbs and stick to fresh fruit, fresh vegetables and whole grain foods for maximum nutritional value.

Sources of complex carbohydrates include:

- Green vegetables
- Starchy vegetables, (including pumpkin, corn, potato, parsnips, squash & sweet potatoes)
- Beans, peas, lentils
- Whole grain foods, (including whole grain pasta, whole grain bread & oatmeal)
- Brown rice

Sources of simple carbohydrates include:

- Yoghurt
- Banana and mango
- 100% fruit juice
- White bread
- White Rice
- Honey
- Milk

Fats

It is important to gain your fat intake from a healthy source rather than fried food and processed saturated fats. Unsaturated fats are the best source for your fat intake. There are two types of unsaturated fats and both have excellent health benefits; monounsaturated fat and polyunsaturated fat. Omega 3 and Omega 6 cannot be produced by our body but are essential when it comes to maintaining the health of our bones.

Sources of unsaturated fats include:

- Salmon
- Mackerel
- Sardines
- Avocado
- Olives
- Olive Oil
- Almonds
- Sesame Oil
- Peanut Oil
- Sunflower seeds
- Hazelnuts
- Peanuts

Protein

For the health and repair of muscles and tendons, protein is an essential requirement in your diet. Always make certain that the source of your protein intake is of a high quality. For a quick post run protein boost add a scoop of whey protein powder to your smoothie or milkshake.

Sources of protein include:

- Tuna
- Chicken
- Nuts
- Eggs
- Beef
- Turkey
- Fish
- Whey Protein Powder
- Cottage Cheese
- Yoghurt

Don't restrict yourself too much, if you never indulge in a tasty dessert, a bar of chocolate or a cool glass of wine every now and again then your will begin to crave those treats. Allow yourself a little pleasure occasionally.

Chapter 7 – Post Run Smoothie Recipes

Banana Smoothie with Chocolate

Ingredients:
1 cup of plain or vanilla yoghurt
¼ cup of milk
1 tsp chocolate powder
1 banana
½ - 1 tsp honey (depending on taste)

Preparation:
Slice banana
Place all ingredients into a blender and blend until smooth

Banana & Vanilla Smoothie with Ginger

Ingredients:
¾ cup vanilla yoghurt
1 banana
½ - 1 tsp fresh grated ginger
1 tbsp honey

Preparation:
Slice banana
Place all ingredients into a blender and blend until smooth

Raspberry & Ginger Smoothie
Ingredients:
1¼ cup raspberries (fresh or frozen)
¾ cup almond milk
2 tsp fresh grated ginger
1½ tbsp honey
1 tsp ground sunflower seeds
2 tsp freshly squeezed lemon juice

Preparation:
Place all ingredients into a blender and blend until smooth

Vanilla & Pineapple Smoothie
Ingredients:
1 cup vanilla yoghurt
6 ice cubes
1 cup chopped pineapple

Preparation:
Place ice cubes into a blender and blend until reduced to small chunks
Add yoghurt and pineapple and blend

Kiwi, Banana & Strawberry Smoothie
Ingredients:
1¼ cup pure apple juice

1 banana

1 medium kiwi

5 medium strawberries

1½ tsp honey

Preparation:
Slice banana and peel and slice kiwi

Place all ingredients into a blender and blend until smooth

Peach & Strawberry Smoothie with Ginger
Ingredients:
1 cup milk

2 tbsp plain or vanilla yoghurt

3 ice cubes

½ cup strawberries

½ cup peaches (fresh or frozen)

¼ tsp fresh grated ginger

2 tsp vanilla whey protein powder

Preparation:
Slice strawberries and peaches

Add milk, yoghurt and ice cubes to the blender and blend until ice has broken down to small chunks

Add whey protein powder and ginger and blend

Add strawberries and peaches and blend until smooth

Berry & Pineapple Smoothie
Ingredients:
1 cup vanilla yoghurt
¾ cup pure pineapple juice
½ cup raspberries (fresh or frozen)
½ cup strawberries (fresh or frozen)

Preparation:
Add raspberries and strawberries to blender and blend to a puree
Add pineapple juice and yoghurt to blender and blend until smooth

Banana & Avocado Smoothie

Ingredients:
250ml Almond Milk
1 tbsp smooth peanut butter
25g baby spinach leaves
½ a banana
50g avocado

Preparation:
Chop banana, avocado and baby spinach leaves and place into the blender. Blend until it becomes mushy
Add almond milk and peanut butter and blend until smooth

Banana Smoothie with Walnuts

Ingredients:
2 cups milk
1 banana
¼ tsp vanilla essence
1 tbsp honey
4 walnuts (alternatively you can use 8 almonds or hazelnuts)

Preparation:
Slice banana
Place walnuts in blender and blend to fine pieces
Place the rest of the ingredients into a blender with the walnuts and blend until smooth

Spinach & Banana Smoothie
Ingredients:
2 cups spinach leaves
2 bananas
1 cup pure apple juice

Preparation:
Chop spinach leaves and place in blender until very finely chopped
Slice bananas
Place banana and apple juice into the blender with spinach and blend until smooth

Conclusion

Thank you again for buying this book!

I hope it was able to inspire you to start running and has helped you to understand how to run in a safe, healthy and enjoyable way along with giving you all the information you need to become a successful runner.

The next step is to put into practice everything you have learnt. Invest in some good running shoes and clothing and develop your running so you can have fun, exercise and get fit. Include friends and go running together. Before long you will be an experienced runner who can pass your knowledge onto others.

Finally, if you enjoyed this book, then I'd like to ask you for a favor, would you be kind enough to leave a review for this book on Amazon? It'd be greatly appreciated!

Thank you and good luck!

Printed in Great Britain
by Amazon